ARAM KHATCHATURIAN

SONATA 1961
Piano

Edited by Luise Vosgerchian

Walter P. Naumburg
Professor of Harvard University

ISBN 978-0-7935-9669-0

G. SCHIRMER, Inc.

DISTRIBUTED BY

HAL•LEONARD®
CORPORATION

7777 W. BLUEMOUND RD. P.O. BOX 13819 MILWAUKEE, WI 53213

To the Memory of My Teacher Nikolai Miaskowsky

Sonata
for Piano

Aram Khatchaturian (1961)
Edited by Luise Vosgerchian

I

* For practicing purposes, the thumb may be held.

4

47591

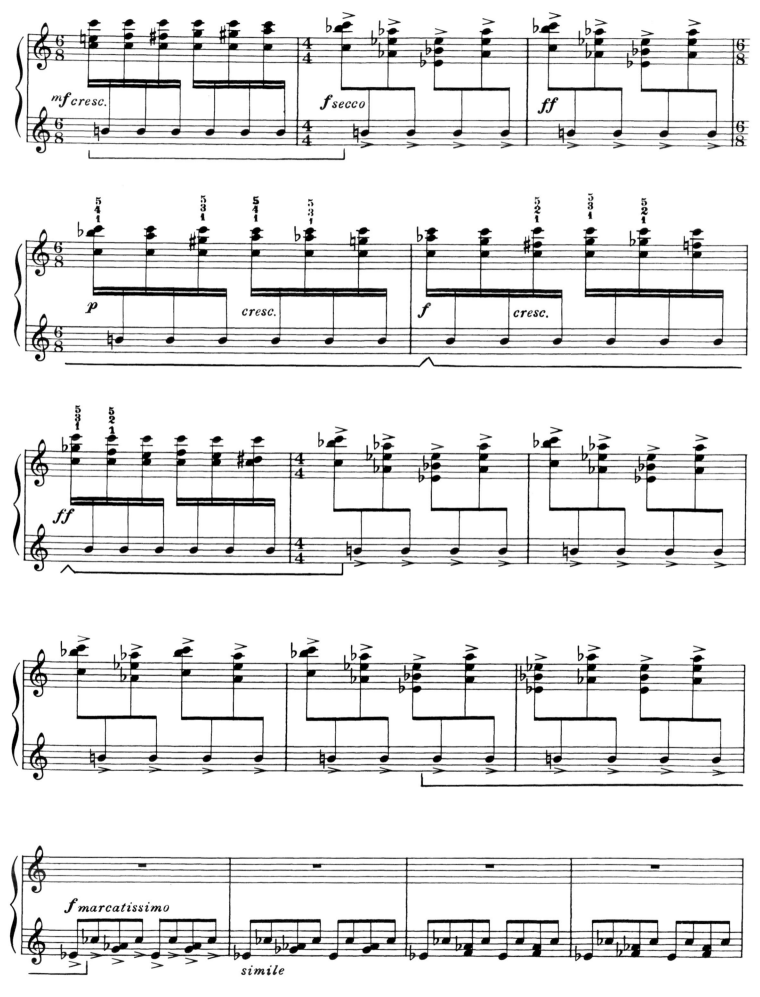

* Using the thumb, make a melodic line with all encircled notes.

47591

II

III